AF732288

Beautiful Pittsburgh

Beautiful
Pittsburgh

Concept and Design: Robert D. Shangle
Text: Andrea Kennet

First Printing October, 1979
Published by Beautiful America Publishing Company
P.O. Box 608, Beaverton, Oregon 97075
Robert D. Shangle, Publisher

Library of Congress Cataloging in Publication Data
Beautiful Pittsburgh
1. Pittsburgh—Description—Views. 1. Kennet, Andrea.
F159.P643B4 974.8'86 79-20481
ISBN 0-89802-088-3
ISBN 0-89802-087-5 (paperback)

Enlarged Prints

Contents

Introduction

Pittsburgh, Pennsylvania defies stereotypes of the industrialized eastern United States. Steeped in a proud heritage, Pittsburgh nestles in a valley surrounded by tree-clad hills and, on the south, by the 600-foot sheer cliff of Mt. Washington in southwestern Pennsylvania, where the Allegheny and Monongahela Rivers join to form the mighty Ohio. Its location at the headwaters of the 987-mile-long Ohio River flung Pittsburgh in the midst of three major historic themes: first as the target for British dominance of the New World during the French and Indian Wars, then as a focus of activity during the colonies' fight for independence, and later as the head of navigation into the vast inland basin during the great migration west.

After its pivotal role in the nation's birth, Pittsburgh settled down to the business of producing steel, a profitable venture fed by the enormous coal beds in the nearby Appalachian Mountains. The city earned success as a major industrial and financial center—and the unfortunate title of "Smoky City." Nowadays, all that is in the past. In the same spirit as their pioneering forefathers, the residents shirked off the grime and smoke, once considered the "badge of prosperity," to create an astonishingly clean city, in defiance of beliefs that progress and grime are a natural combination. Pittsburgh is the producer of one-fifth of the country's steel, a dominant manufacturer of glass, aluminum, and coal refining, and headquarters for 14 major international corporations. But the pollution once associated with the city is gone. Even the steel mills no longer billow the colored smoke that was once the city's trademark.

The dominance of heavy industry creates a virile ambience throughout the city, setting a strong, almost "macho" tone. "Pittsburgh is masculine," comments Patrick Horsbrugh, in his *Pittsburgh Perceived*, a review of the city for Pittsburgh Planning Commission's community renewal program. ". . . its industries set the pace; the buildings commemorate, in four-square strength, the commercial progress of the times. The whole atmosphere is geared to manufacturing, to trading, to education, to things of the future." But the city's cleanliness draws praise even from people who don't usually like cities. "A city of exceptional beauty," praises Horsbrugh, an attribute of which residents remain unself-conscious and have "never indulged in vulgar advertisement nor extravagant exposure, nor flamboyant costume in a flagrant attempt to attract attention."

The Renaissance, as people dub the rejuvenation of the city, was accomplished quietly, effectively, and nearly within a decade. Residents maintain a wry chuckle for visitors, who head toward the industrial center without enthusiasm, only to discover urban charm. To tell the truth, the average resident can't imagine that anyone would *not* fall in love with the city. Pittsburghers have no worry about old taunts by outsiders about the then-justified, but hated, nickname of "Smoky City" of pre-World War II. An atmosphere of back-patting is evident. Some of it is by outsiders, such as environmentalists, who hail Pittsburgh as the perfect test case of cleansing a city, or, by the many journalists attracted by the transformation of a city of "unbelievable ugliness to shining beauty in less than half a generation," as described by *Holiday* magazine writer Herbert Kubly.

Some of the back-patting is among residents who are understandably proud of the shining city and its history. Plaques are mounted on walls or erected on posts and inscribed with tales about people, places, or events that played a role in the country's making. It's not unusual to find a brass name plate on one side of a downtown department store's entry and another plaque on the other side of the door giving a bit of the history of the building.

Much of Pittsburgh's beauty comes not only from the numerous 100 and 200-year-old buildings, but from the fact that they are used. Horsbrugh was attracted by the emphasis on preservation and remarked in his review of the city that its attractiveness "is one of natural inheritance . . . it survives and is as available as ever for anyone who will pause to perceive." Four 19th-century churches in downtown are marked historic landmarks and still house worship services. The Allegheny County Courthouse and Jail, in its late 1800s Romanesque grandeur, a bit reminiscent of a medieval fortress, is still used for its original purpose. An arched causeway connects the masonry structures high above the streets, and is dubbed the "bridge of sighs" in an empathy with prisoners who cross the trestle from court to cell.

Although an excellent modern bus service connects downtown and the suburbs, commuters often prefer the old trolleys, rickety, uncomfortable relics that glide over cobblestone and paved streets and clatter their ways into the hearts of Pittsburghers.

When the food processing family, the Heinzes, gifted the city with a cultural center, it was natural to remodel the old Penn Theater from its rococco obsolesence into Heinz Hall for the Performing Arts, a mixture of baroque grandeur and modern acoustics. The Pittsburgh Symphony Orchestra, Opera, and Civic Light Opera make their home there amidst a myriad of musical and dramatic events.

An old cemetery in the center of downtown would be incongruous in any other city. Trinity Burial Ground, located between Trinity Episcopal Cathedral and First Presbyterian Church, is the oldest unreconstructed city landmark. Once a full block with 4,000 graves, progress has whittled away the burial ground to a handful of gravestones and grassy patch between the two 19th-century churches. Once an Indian burial ground and cemetery for the French and British forts, the burial ground is the resting place of many historic figures including Red Pole, principal chief of the Shawnee nation.

Considering this habit of mixing new with old, it is not surprising the city is often described as a place of unexpected combinations. The sleek lines of the 64-story U.S. Steel building, tallest between Chicago and New York when erected in 1970, shares the horizon with the gingerbread facade of the old Union Trust building. Alcoa's unique aluminum-sheathed headquarters rivals for attention with the black open-metal steeple of the old Smithfield Congregational Church built in 1925.

The physical setting of the city presents a contrast of pictures. From the north, the rural entry provides an idyllic setting. Travelers from the south are surprised with a sudden, breathtaking view of the Golden Triangle as their vehicles emerge from Fort Pitt Tunnel. The masculine atmosphere described by the city reviewer permeates the eastern entry along the momentous Monongahela entry, passing the Jones and Laughlin (J&L) steel mills. The Ohio River opens from a tranquil, leisurely pace beneath the West End Bridge to reveal the Golden Triangle as an aquatic city.

In an acrobatic twist, Pittsburgh manages to turn around an old adage and balance a haystack on top of a needle. Concentrated in the one-half mile square Golden Triangle, heart of the city, are major corporate headquarters and employment, education, dining, shopping, and evening entertainments easily within walking distance to suit a metropolitan population of two million people. The close proximity of work and culture in the Golden triangle makes Pittsburgh a city on its feet, literally. Once downtown, either by trolley, bus, or private motor vehicle, everything a person could desire is at hand, or at foot.

When 21-year-old George Washington spied the Point during a 1753 exploration, he remarked that the land at the headwaters of the Ohio River appeared more than suitable for a primary fort. Little did he envision the magnitude of the role the Point would play. Pittsburgh begins the booming, industrial belt that stretches westward across the Great Lakes plains to Chicago and Milwaukee.

Point State Park, at the apex of the Golden Triangle, its fountain spouting 150 feet into the sky, and 36 acres of manicured lawn, promenade, and remnants of Fort Pitt, reigns as the city's symbol. Homefolk wade in the fountain, lunch along the promenade and view the coal-laden barges on the Monongahela, or just stroll about to reflect and stretch. Pleasure boats often dock along the Point, providing a twinkling regatta of lights at dusk.

A few years ago, the Point was mud, water, and commercial sprawl, but in a fairy-tale like transformation it has become the city's most popular gathering spot. The park retains some of the past as the site of the original Fort Pitt, named after William Pitt, Earl of Catham. A six-sided oak block house, built in 1764, and two of the five original bastions—one serves as a museum—have been restored.

It is the Point that inspired the phrase, many years earlier, "I am smith of land and sea," and the steel industry, the strain, ". . . monarch of all the forges," in the 19th century Hymn of Pittsburgh by Richard Realt.

The rivers pour life into Pittsburgh. Described aptly as "the city (that) rises out of the rivers" by one of the local newspapers, Pittsburgh relies on the rivers to provide sources for economic growth and recreation. The rivers are as moody as the seasons—a playground for boaters in summer and a racetrack for ice floes in winter. White caps dance on the surface during high winds and storms, while mists rise from the waters on the dawn of a clear day.

The Allegheny River, its Indian name meaning "stream of the Cave People," provides the arena for most of the recreational boating. Industry freight travels the Monongahela, "high banks falling down" in Indian and "The Mon" among local folks; and barges play the Ohio, whose name comes from a Delaware word meaning "white with frothing water."

The rivers spawn local folklore and heroes such as the fighting riverman Mike Fink in the mid-1800s and, more recently, Captain Frederick Way Jr., pilot, boat-builder, and writer, who attained legendary status as captain of the fastest packet boat of his time. Pittsburgh gave birth to the first steamboat on inland waters in 1811, Robert Fulton's *New Orleans*. The most magnificent steamboat was the Gothic beauty, *The Great Republic*, whose career was ill-fated from her launch in 1867. She bankrupted her first owners and burned a few years later.

The rivers crown Pittsburgh as the nation's largest inland port. Tugboats power barges from the coal mills to the steel factories. Crews work 30-day shifts on the waters and become landlubbers the next month. Forty-six dams manipulate the turbulent waters which once posed a constant flooding threat, until the St. Patrick's Day Flood in 1936 convinced city leaders and citizens to control the torrents.

A need to ford the rivers prompted Pittsburgh to construct bridges, some 500 of them, according to bridge expert and author Elizabeth Herberton, and enough to earn for Pittsburgh the title of ''City of Bridges.'' Major tunnels pierce through the hillsides to give access from the suburbs to downtown. Two inclines, relics of the past, continue to operate, partially because of the people's affections for them and because residents on top of the hills rely on them as alternate transportation. Visitors and residents equally enjoy nighttime rides for the view of the city.

No book about Pittsburgh can ignore an explanation of the riddle of the city's unique spelling. Any Pittsburgher worth his steel will insist that Pittsburgh with a final 'h' is the original and proper spelling, unlike the Pittsburgs in California, Kansas, Illinois, or Texas.

The name designation and the 'h' were first applied by the British General, John Forbes, when he sent the notice of victory to William Penn regarding the take over of Fort Ligonier from the French. On November 27, 1758, he announced that the new name of the fort was Fort Pitt, and the settlement was ''Pittsborough.'' The borough spelling was common in Forbes' homeland, Scotland.

The final 'h' was lost unwillingly when, in a quest for standardization, the United States Board of Geographic Names stripped the final consonant in 1891. Places pronounced 'berg' would be spelled 'burg,' ruled the board. Perserverance among local citizens, who waged a strong battle in legislature, won back the 'h' in 1911 when the United States Geographic Board, successor to the geographic names board, voted back the consonant. Senator George T. Oliver, a leader in the quest and publisher of the *Pittsburgh Gazette Times*, published the triumphant announcement of the adoption of the final 'h' by the federal government. The opposing *Pittsburgh Press* held out for about 20 years against the restored letter.

The 'h' is highly regarded by Pittsburghers. ''It symbolizes our individuality, our special quality as a city,'' explains author James Van Trump some years later in an essay about the controversial spelling.

Another tradition ingrained in Pittsburgh is building parks. Most of the parks are the result of a philanthropic bent among the city's wealthy. Considering the spacious parks that sprawl throughout the north, east, south, and west sides, it's not surprising that much leisure time is spent outdoors. Parks appear to be used at all hours, as is the downtown, in an unusual mix of urban life and a desire for nature.

Flowers, fountains, and greenways replace the monotony of concrete downtown in parks such as Mellon Square, named after brothers Andrew and Richard of the

Mellon family banking dynasty, Equitable Plaza in Gateway Center and Point State Park. Sophisticated executives are often spied dipping bared feet in one of the many fountains, or, coatless, tieless, with shirt sleeves rolled, basking in the sun during a hot summer day on a respite from the fast-paced work day.

Pittsburgh parks share a common scheme of rolling broad lawns, clipped and manicured, a sprinkling of flower beds, cozy groves of deciduous trees whose leaves paint a rainbow of colors the most skilled artist would envy, and the inevitable fountains and statues. Roadways curve through the parks and walking paths meander through the greenery. Yet, in some manner, either by man-made recreation facilities or physical setting, each park retains a sense of individuality.

Perhaps the most amazing and beautiful of the city parks is Schenley Park, in Oakland, abutting University of Pittsburgh and Carnegie Institute. Pittsburgh profited when 15-year-old Mary Grohan, granddaughter of wealthy capitalist James O'Hara, eloped with soldier Captain Edward Schenley, twice widowed and nearly thrice his bride's age. Her controversial marriage to a poorer and older man set tongues wagging and split the family. Legal battles ensued until Mrs. Schenley reclaimed her estate, and donated 300 acres in Oakland in 1889 for a park. She also gave the aged block house on Point State Park to the Daughters of the American Revolution.

Ever since the first municipal band concert there in 1911, Schenley Park has hosted numerous summer movies and music productions on its grassy slopes. Its wide variety of attractions rates it high in popularity. Its location by University of Pittsburgh and its educational and medical facilities make it but a short walk from the toil of books or from the medicinal aura of health clinics. The view from the top of the hill in Schenley Park gives a splendid panorama of the city, three rivers and many hills, which is a good reason why so many residents gather there to watch the sun set over the city.

Panther Hollow Lake in Schenley Park recalls a bout between man and nature in pioneering years. In the 1760s, a hunt was organized to drive out a feared panther. Today, a much tamer Schenley Park is home for the Phipps Conservatory and its myriad of plantings. A nature museum, golf course, hiking trails, and tennis courts provide a varied playground.

Carnegie Institute, donated to the city by Andrew Carnegie, is among features that gained University of Pittsburgh prominence. The institute was part of Carnegie's effort to share his money with the public before his death. The huge stone building houses the city's major library, music hall, art gallery, and museum of natural science. Carnegie was known for his spree of library giving. According to the accepted story, he remembered his earlier, penniless years of book borrowing and built free libraries so that others would have the benefit of bettering themselves through reading.

Additions of the Sarah Scaife Gallery and the Heinz Galleries in the 1970s provided desperately needed expansion for the Carnegie Institute Museum of Art. The first gallery has been acclaimed by the *New York Times* as an ''unflawed paradise'' for its airy spaces suffused with natural light, providing a congenial setting for paintings and sculptures. A large glass wall overlooks a sculpture court and fountain plaza. Named for Sarah Scaife, sister of Richard K. Mellon, the gallery opened in 1974.

Carnegie Museum of Natural History earned prominence as the ''home of the dinosaurs'' for its extended collection of the early land inhabitants' skeletons: exhibits include more than 10,000 objects. Lifelike dioramas of wild animals in natural surroundings depict not only a world of animals most people don't see, but a high quality of taxidermy in practice.

A short drive east on Forbes Avenue to Squirrel Hills, again a neighborhood named for an abundance of that particular creature, is Frick Park, a contrast to other city parks because of its wilderness and emphasis on nature. No roadways go into the park, instead, footpaths lead through the deciduous and evergreen woods.

Smaller parks and playgrounds dot the residential areas, including Westinghouse and Mellon parks, which pay tribute to two of the city's great industrialists.

Allegheny—an old-time designation for the area to the north and across the river from downtown, which is now called North Side—was the site of one of the city's first major urban renewal projects in the 1960s. The community benefited by the construction of Allegheny Center, a complex of offices, townhouses, and shops around a public square. Greenways surround the modern civic center. The Old Post Office, Carnegie Free Library, and numerous older buildings stand restored among the new creations of urban redevelopment. A statue of a partially-draped woman, a monument to Allegheny city civil war soldiers, overlooks descendants of the fighters as they wade and splash in man-made Lake Elizabeth. The outlying park is home for exotic birds in the Aviary and the Soldiers and Sailors Memorial.

Along the north shore of the Allegheny River stretches Roberto Clemente Memorial Park, a natural gathering spot for river watchers and pilots of pleasure craft. The park ends just short of Three Rivers Stadium.

Further north and west is Riverside Park where stargazers get a heavenly view of the skies through a 116-foot telescope at the white-domed Allegheny Observatory. The sky is not the limit of attractions: Perrys Athletic Field, adjacent to the park, offers sporting events.

Pittsburghers have a habit of naming communities and parks for compass directions with downtown as the base. North Park and South Park, enormous dedications of public open space, are aptly just out of the city in the proper directions. North Park wraps around Marshall and North Park lakes. Live deer roam and a "fountain of youth" at the park makes it a natural site for Girl Scout and Boy Scout cabins. Athletic fields and courts for all seasons, golf courses and swimming pools are attractions shared by North and South parks. South Park, without lakes, hosts the Allegheny County Fairgrounds and game preserve, as a kind of compensation.

Within less than a 75-mile radius from Pittsburgh is a great contrast in scenery: green glens along the rivers, rural, white-glove-neat farms and more elegant reminders of the past. North, past Fox Chapel, is the magnificent Tudor estate of Hartwood Acres, now dedicated to the public. Southeast on Route 40 is a breathtaking tour of Laurel Caverns, artistically altered by man, in the Laurel Highlands, as well as the excitement of rafting and kayaking on the turbulent white-waters of Youghioheny River at Ohiopyle. Nearby in Bear Run is Falling-water, the summer home of the Pittsburgh department store family, the Kaufmanns. Designed by Frank Lloyd Wright, the house is built over and around a cascading waterfall: an arresting effort to preserve, yet use and enjoy, natural beauty.

The Golden Triangle

Shrewd forethought overruled a minority desire to build Fort Pitt on McKees Rocks, where the Ohio Company of Virginia had begun erecting the original outpost, in early 1754. The French, who seized the fort two months later, foresaw the Point as a more strategic position. The British army that felled Fort Dusquene—and renamed it Pitt—agreed.

Ever since, land at the confluence of the two rivers, the Golden Triangle, has served as the heart of Pittsburgh. First it was the shipping port for the farms and then for the industry that sprang up rapidly after the War of 1812. In the mid-1800s, as Pittsburgh turned in its plows for steel forges, the Golden Triangle took on a new character with increased production and population. Accomplishments were many, but the result gave English author Charles Dickens the impression of "an ugly confusion of backs of buildings and crazy galleries and stairs."

The Point has always been the focus of the half-mile square city center, both for its beauty and its navigational advantages. It is natural that Point State Park and its 150-foot fountain, fed by a fourth mysterious underground river, basks in favor of both visitors and residents. But the Point only begins the conglomeration of business and industry, churches and residences, restaurants, theaters, and entertainment places that jostle each other for room and attention in the triangle.

Using Point State Park as a geographical landmark, move eastward along Liberty Avenue past the originals of The Renaissance, Gateway Center, and Equitable Plaza gardens. Further east rise the most recent products of The Renaissance, the Oliver Plaza buildings.

Just one block southeast, on Sixth Avenue, two monarchs of established religion contrast strikingly with the newness of Oliver Plaza and Gateway Center. The First Presbyterian Church and Trinity Episcopal Cathedral fence in the Old Trinity Burial Ground where many of Pittsburgh's pioneers rest.

East on Sixth are more city landmarks that illustrate the thriving difference between Pittsburgh and other large cities. Mellon Square is bordered on one side by the Alcoa building. The 31-story, 410-foot structure, built in 1952, was the world's first aluminum skyscraper; only the structure's frame is steel. Surrounding buildings exemplify other construction styles of passing popularity—The William Penn Hotel and Union Trust Co. Building, both old and ornate, stand next to the modern Mellon Bank Building.

The U.S. Steel building towers further east on Sixth. It is known as "the tallest building until Chicago." The 64-story skyscraper is built over the obsolete Pennsylvania Railroad tunnel and is equipped with an underground terminal in case a rail commuter system should be revived.

Southward of the steel headquarters stand the imposing and massive Allegheny County Courthouse and Jail, squatting over two blocks at Grant and Forbes. The courthouse and jail were built in the 19th century in defiance of the rising technology of metal frame buildings. Instead, the buildings are classic examples of the Romanesque style made popular by architect H.H. Richardson in the late 1800s. It won recognition as one of the most magnificent buildings erected in America during that century.

An old farmer's market area further west on Forbes has been turned into Market Square, a block of greenery and fountain, yet another break from downtown concrete. Heinz Hall, cultural center of Pittsburgh and home of its music, stands at Penn Avenue and Sixth.

One block north along Sixth Street, industry shares the waters of Allegheny River, popular with pleasure craft. Pittsburgh's many bridges provide a myriad of spectacular sites, but one of the most pleasing is visible from the south bank of the Allegheny. The "Trilogy of Bridges" is composed of the Sixth, Seventh, and Ninth street bridges, all self-anchored eye-bar suspension bridges with center spans that exceed 400 feet and stretch more than 1,200 feet in length.

A useful eastern boundary to the Golden Triangle is formed by Bigelow Boulevard and Crosstown Boulevard, major arteries that pass interests such as the Conrail Railroad Station at Eleventh and Liberty and the Civic Arena. Dusquene University overlooks the commerce center from "The Bluff."

The Renaissance

People tend to nurture a fondness, in some cases almost a patriotic fervor, for the places they call home. In earlier times this manifested itself as a love of the land, but nowadays, with the land virtually overrun and most Americans living in cities, people are likely to be attached to the works of man that dominate their environment: bridges, streets, buildings. This can present some difficulties when the home you love is not particularly loveable—as was the case in Pittsburgh before the Renaissance.

Pittsburgh, in a trend typical of the United States, for the first couple of centuries concentrated on its accomplishments and ignored its environment. Disasters created by the strain of industry on nature finally awoke the realization that man cannot live and prosper if he can't breathe the air of his habitat or if aquatic life is nonexistent in his waters. Anecdotes about the smog and grime began to take a toil on Pittsburghers' tolerance. Businessmen acquired the custom of changing their white shirts at noon because the sooty air discolored them. Cars often drove through the city with lights turned on at high noon.

An intense hatred for the jesting slurs about the grime and nickname of "Smoky City," combined with the realization that Pittsburgh was fast becoming a disagreeable habitat for humans and animals, spawned the Renaissance, the rejuvenation of the city. Political prejudices were cast aside. Mayor David L. Lawrence, leader of the Democrats, and Republican leader and banking magnate Richard King Mellon joined forces to lead city officials, industry, and residents in cleansing the city. Smoke and water pollution were easily targeted as main barriers to a necessary economic rebirth of the city, and talk of solutions began prior to World War II. A smoke control ordinance drafted in 1943, was sidelined by the needs of military production. Anti-pollution measures were postponed only as long as the war lasted. Once government powers enacted the delayed smoke abatement ordinance in 1946, Mellon and the community of industrialists and financiers stood behind their traditional rivals—Lawrence and city politicians—to force compliance by those less than enthusiastic.

Downtown Pittsburgh from the north bank of the Allegheny River
(Following pages) First Presbyterian Church

MEDIAN SCHOOL OF ALLIED HEALTH
PENN TECHNICAL INSTITUTE
GOODYEAR

Downtown district from Mt. Washington
(Preceding pages) Looking east along the Monongahela from Mt. Washington

Allegheny Observatory, Riverview Park

Equitable Plaza, Gateway Center
(Following pages) Point State Park, downtown from Mt. Washington

Fountain, Point State Park

HILTON

Carnegie Library
(Preceding pages) Point State Park from Roberto Clemente Memorial Park

Point State Park

LANDMARKS
SQUARE
OLD
POST OFFICE
SHOP
OPEN

Mellon Square
(Following pages) Downtown Pittsburgh

Old Post Office in Landmarks Square

ALLEGHENY CENTER
CLARK

HILTON

Allegheny County Soldiers' Memorial
(Preceding pages) Provincial Hall, LaRoche College

Phipps Conservatory, Schenley Park

Equitable Plaza, Gateway Center

(Following pages) Three Rivers Stadium, Point State Park Fountain

Mellon Square, Smithfield Congregational Church

ALLEGHENY CENTER

Mellon Square Fountain

(Preceding pages) Three Rivers Stadium, Point State Park. Ft. Duquesne bridge in background, Ft. Pitt bridge foreground.

Masonic Temple

Equitable Plaza, Gateway Center

(Following pages) Downtown Pittsburgh from Mt. Washington

Phipps Conservatory, Schenley Park

IN GOD WE TRUST
SHIELDS RUBBER CORP

Cathedral of Learning, University of Pittsburgh
(Preceding pages) Downtown from south bank of Monongahela River

Panther Hollow Lake, Schenley Park

Garden at Duquesne University
(Following pages) Downtown from Mt. Washington

Carnegie Free Library, built in 1890

U.S. Steel Building from Duquesne University

Downtown at Sunset from Schenley Park

When a major railroad company balked, Mellon, a true capitalist, calmly informed the transportation company that official Mellon interests could take business elsewhere. Not surprising, in light of the vast Mellon industrial empire, the railroad company dropped its objections. (Mellon interests control Gulf Oil, Koppers, and Alcoa and maintain dominant influences on other corporations such as U.S. Steel, Westinghouse, Pennsylvania Railroad, Pittsburgh Plate Glass and Pittsburgh Consolidation Coal).

Cooperation, most voluntary but some through such persuading pressure, ended use of soft coal by households; railroads and shops shifted from steam to diesel power; and coal mining operations found better methods to eliminate waste. Then the path was clear for physical esthetic improvements.

Renewal of the Golden Triangle from grime to true corporate ''gold'' aptly began at the Triangle's apex at the confluence of the rivers, where Pittsburgh began two centuries before. Since 1806 when Hugh Brackenridge suggested the ''finest gardens in the world may be formed'' on the land between the rivers, fruitless talk had been devoted to constructing a park at the Point. Instead, the pinnacle of land was left to an ugly conglomerate of warehouses, urban blight and railroad trackage that buried the old Blockhouse. The ''Moses Plan'' drawn by planner Robert Moses, called for that park to become a reality during the Renaissance, and an historic park was begun in 1945 with the cooperation of state officials.

As the 36 acres of condemned buildings were cleared for Point State Park, corporations answered a need for modern facilities with the creation of Gateway Center at the base of the park. The Wabash Terminal and objecting store owners proved sizeable obstacles to construction of the Gateway complex, but the businessmen were reassured, and a fire destroyed the terminal in March, 1946, to literally clear the way for Gateway Center. Equitable Life Assurance Society led the way by erecting four silvery buildings, followed by the Hilton Hotel, Gateway Towers luxury apartments, The Westinghouse Center, and Equitable Plaza park.

The breathtaking pace of urban renewal gave Pittsburgh a bombed-out appearance as old was bulldozed down to make way for new. Gateway Center sparked similar activity throughout the city. Substandard housing in the Lower Hill area gave way to the Civic Arena that boasts of a retractable-domed roof. A full block was transformed from a lot to an underground garage for 900 vehicles and topped with paving, greenery, and fountain as Mellon Square Park. The park is dedicated to the memory of brothers Andrew W., and Richard B. Mellon, who cajoled, worked, and paid the city in its earlier years, built with funding from three Mellon family foundations at a cost of more than $4,500,000. Complaints that the park would waste valuable commercial property space was quelled when the finished park was quickly adopted by downtown workers as a gathering place for lunches and coffee breaks.

Activity grew beyond the borders of the Golden Triangle. The Civic Arena capped the Lower Hill Redevelopment Program at Washington. The 450-foot diameter roof of the steel building consists of eight pie-shaped sectors, six of which are moveable to make the world's largest retractable dome. Department store monarch Edgar Kaufmann dreamed for many years of a well-constructed amphitheater for his city. When the aging Dusquene Gardens closed, leaving Pittsburgh without an arena, Kaufmann donated $1-1½ million toward a replacement. His generosity meshed well with The Renaissance and the desire to replace substandard housing in the Lower Hill area. Some 1,200 families relocated, and ground was broken in 1962 for the $20 million Washington Plaza Apartment plan and 19-story Catham Center, along with the Civic Arena.

Pace of the Renaissance slackened and renewal continues at a more subtle walk. The third phase, as some locals see current work, concentrates on Grant Street, the county courthouse and jail. Phase four, if there is such a step, will head further inland still. Grassroots efforts continue as well, although not with the rapid speed of the beginning, when residents washed and painted their homes in a general sprucing up. Instead, repair is at a more individual rate.

The minute-by-minute, seemingly overnight, changes of The Renaissance in the 1950s and 60s have passed in favor of a leveling off. Some residents mourn the lost spirit of early Renaissance. Others have adjusted their expectations to a slower pace. Others have grown accustomed to the changes and take them for granted. After all, the sky and blight has been scoured, rivers cleansed, flood-control measures taken, and dams now harness the rivers. Modernistic buildings pierce the horizon. But residents want more. The Renaissance shuffles under the prodding of Pittsburghers who view their accomplishments with ''pride tinged with impatience that more can be done—and is,'' as aptly stated by the *Pittsburgh Quote*'s tenth anniversary issue.

Neighborhoods

Early Pittsburghers had to look no further than the coal-fired melting-pots of their steel and glass mills to discover a metaphor to describe the population of their rapidly-growing industrial city. The melting pot syndrome hit Pittsburgh just before the 20th century. Early residents had shared the same European cultural backgrounds, immigrating mostly to the southwestern Pennsylvania growing metropolis from Scotland, Wales, Ireland, Germany, and England. But an immigration wave in the 1880s brought groups of quite different origins. Arriving with high hopes to labor in the glass factories, steel mills and coal mines were Hungarians, Poles, Estonians, Latvians, Czechs, Greeks, and Armenians, many sharing a Slavic heritage.

Those early ethnic roots are visible today throughout Pittsburgh. Neighborhoods sporting names of particular nationalities on storefronts and residential mailboxes illustrate a tendency of similar cultures to settle together. The old religions and customs survive American standardization, the best example being the churches. A half dozen Catholic churches may huddle within a few blocks of each other, close in proximity but differing in the nationalities they serve: Ukranian, Bulgarian, or Italian. Some radio stations schedule broadcasts geared to different nationalities. Programs vary from Jewish, Polish, Italian, and Greek, to the more exotic tongues of Croatian, Lithuanian, Serbian, and Slovenian. Festivals throughout the warmer seasons celebrate the different heritages and share the good times with others. Each year a green stripe down certain streets announces St. Patrick's Day on March 17, when the Irish and just about everybody else pay homage to the mythical patron saint of Ireland.

Much of the tight-knit community style settling remains visible. At one time business, residences, and industry shared the Golden Triangle, but as all three elements of the city grew, so did the size of the urban setting. Bridges and tunnels eased access to the neighboring hillsides and sparked sprawling neighborhoods.

East of the Golden Triangle, two neighborhoods present a great contrast. The Hill area, nestled between downtown and Oakland, struggles against the blight of substandard housing. It contains some remarkable relics, albiet decaying, of 19th-century row-housing and tenements. The community thrives with social interaction and life in spite of its deprived appearance. A few blocks up the slope, hilly Oakland is the site of the University of Pittsburgh that presents a pandemonium of music, arts, education, parks, its medical center, the Carnegie Institute and Schenley Park. Its residential section claims a moneyed past and was hailed in 1899 as "the most beautiful suburb in the world," by an immodest Pittsburgh Board of Trade.

Grass root organizations voiced demands at town hall meetings for a comprehensive renewal program to restore neighboring East Liberty to its former position as the "hub" of the city's East End. New life has been breathed into East Liberty by its residents, giving the community the status as the "neighborhood that dared." The Omego Street Group, a loose nomenclature of 11 property owners who trace their origins to the same Italian hamlet, exemplifies the local struggle against all odds to keep neighborhoods intact hand-in-hand with urban renewal. The Omego Group has slowly acquired and rehabilitated rundown properties with help from a government agency.

Across the Monongahela River, southeast from downtown, lies some of Pittsburgh's traditionally desired real estate and historic land. Homestead was once a separate city spawned by the Bessemer Steel Plant. A splendid view of downtown and the rivers from atop Mount Washington gives properties further west a special status. Village-like communities cover the slope between South Side and Allentown on Mount Oliver, similar to those on Mount Washington where some wonderful restaurants share the view. Each of the communities share a common design with their identity spelled through the principal feature of the neighborhood, the churches.

Southside, a little older, retains its grace against the more magnificent homes on Mount Washington and Mount Oliver. Onion-shaped steeples in place of the traditional pinnacles that usually top American churches reflect the Hungarian and Bulgarian ancestry of residents. Houses and other buildings huddle close to each other. Old though the neighborhoods are, residents are proud of the maintenance of their homes and streets. Narrow stairs, rowhousing, and cobblestone roads give the Southside a special flavor.

A little further out are the neighborhoods of Greentree, Mount Lebanon, and Castle Shannon, each similar to other Pittsburgh communities but with individual traits that make the neighborhoods so attractive.

West of downtown along the Ohio River are McKees Rocks, which house a mixture of ethnic heritages. The hills were used as an Indian burial ground for centuries and covers three layers of burial sites dating from 3000 B.C. to 1500 A.D.

Great sentimental and historic attachment are connected with North Side, which spreads from the shores of the Ohio and Allegheny Rivers to the inland hills. The idiom ''North Side'' hardly describes the color and position once held by the area that encompasses the former city of Allegheny and its neighborhoods. Residents abhor the title of North Side out of a dislike for Allegheny's present status as an appendage to Pittsburgh.

Incorporated by Pittsburgh in 1907, Old Allegheny and its surrounding colorful neighborhoods hosted some of Pittsburgh area's more elegant and gracious living until its decline in the 1900s. The area typifies late 19th century residential neighborhoods that developed in many industrial cities and deteriorated through the mid-twentieth. Society Hill now houses a community college in contrast to the leisure life it once nurtured.

North Side's Old Allegheny entails neighborhoods, unique in their identities, of North Shore, Old Allegheny's riverfront; Central North Side, the heart of Old Allegheny and its commons; East North Side, once Dutchtown, a commercial center where German and English were both taught in public schools until 1925; Allegheny West and its remarkable townhouses; Manchester, once a solid upper middle-class suburb; Perry Hilltop and Fineview, with finer yards and view; and Troy Hill and its German village layout.

The architecture of the area is as complex, varied, and interesting as the city itself, ranging from Federal style and Greek Revival pediment and pilaster works seen on the Old Widows Home on Armandale, to the pretentious Italianate style of Manchester or Perry Hilltop. Stained glass, often Tiffany, turrets, and ornate facades turn plain brick box-like homes into works of art.

Old Allegheny conjures up the largest nostalgic lump in the throats of oldtime Pittsburghers. Organized several years after Pittsburgh's founding in 1759, Allegheny was slow to mature chiefly because of frequent Indian traffic in the area and due to a strange twist in claims by Pennsylvania and Virginia to the Pittsburgh area until Congress solved the issue after the Revolution. The area was part of a 3,000-acre reservation tract to meet the state's obligations to its war veterans.

Incorporated in 1840, Allegheny included all the amenities of early urban living through such institutions as Allegheny Market House, Boggs and Buhl department store, Ober Park and its magnificent fountain, Lake Elizabeth, the Music Hall of Allegheny Library and the Heinz plant. University of Pittsburgh opened in 1882 at Buena Vista and Perrysville before moving to Oakland in 1900.

The old grandeur is gone except for rowhousing, deteriorated but marked for restoration, and some of the buildings from the old commons, thanks to the

Pittsburgh Historic and Landmarks Foundation. Mixed amongst the modern stores, professional buildings, and parking garages at Allegheny Center is the Old Post Office Museum, the city post office from 1894 to 1897. It is now a museum and headquarters for the historical foundation. Allegheny Center was built on the site of the old Allegheny Commons in an effort to restore both the city and its spirit. The Old Post Office, Market Square, and the first Carnegie Public Library share the new commons.

Pittsburgh's ethnic heritage is best illustrated in Allegheny. English descendants settled in Old Allegheny town with the Commons; Scottish and Irish lived westward in Manchester. Germans settled eastward in Dutchtown at the southern end of East Street. Ethnic division continued there as the Germans inhabited inland areas and the Swiss lived in Swiss Hole by the Allegheny shores.

Four distinct neighborhoods remain intact surrounding the Allegheny Commons on the north, west, and east. Central North Side has been the most stable community and has been revitalized to a great degree through a block program. The Mexican War Streets on the other side of West Park were laid out around 1850, their street names associated with the war that was then current. Like surrounding communities, the Mexican War Streets were built by the industrial rich and reflect the individual builder's tastes. The homes were gradually converted into rooming houses as the upper-income residents moved to the eastern and northern suburbs in the early 1900s. Allegheny West is of similar date and character, filled with mid- and late-Victorian houses.

Manchester, just west of Allegheny West, sports sprawling lawns compared to the tight, brick housing of Allegheny. New styles and the larger lawns spawned some Italian Villa and Queen Anne architecture. The area was built in 1860 first by Jewish merchants and then German businessmen.

Perry Hilltop, overlooking central Allegheny, is a chain of neighborhoods strung together along Perrysville Avenue. Some structures date as far back as 1850, but main construction began in 1900 when trolley service started. Some of the best samples of Colonial Revival houses dress Perrysville Avenue. Nearby Fineview and East Street Valley abut, similar in grid-plan design and architecture.

Troy Hill, settled in the mid-nineteenth century, is a compact, stable community with the aura of a medieval hill town, and still predominantly German Catholic. Spring Hill, between Troy Hill and East Street, is another generally German community, with housing erected from 1850 to 1920.

A History of Innovative Transportation

Pittsburgh's location at the headwaters of the Ohio River proved strategic militarily, but the surrounding hills and three rivers were a headache to early residents who wanted in or out of town. As floods motivated merchants to head further inland in the Golden Triangle, wealthy residents sought refuge on the hillsides. Problems of crossing the rivers or climbing the steep hillsides served as barriers to transportation only long enough to inspire innovative solutions.

The Allegheny and Monongahela Rivers formed watery boundaries on the north and south of the city, the Ohio River on the west. Ferry boats initially provided the desired transportation with ease between Pittsburgh and settlements such as Allegheny City. Growing industry and population demanded better access. So in 1810 the first steps toward erecting bridges were made with a charter for two bridges over the Allegheny and Monongahela Rivers. The Allegheny bridge to Allegheny City opened in 1820 and the Monongahela bridge, near Smithfield Street, in 1818, both the typical toll spans of covered wooden construction. The 1845 fire that destroyed one-third of the city torched the Monongahela bridge, opening the way for some inventive ideas.

A German, John A. Roebling, brought his plans for suspension bridges to Pittsburgh, after Prussian engineers rejected his ideas as impractical. His design replaced the burned-out bridge over the Monongahela River and served 35 years before being replaced in 1833 with an efficient utilitarian structure designed by his son. Hailed as the "forerunner of the famous Berkeley Bridge," the 1833 version of the Smithfield Street bridge bore a sign warning against vibrations and instructing processions to cross the bridge without music.

Stories and some true history give each of Pittsburgh's bridges character beyond the utilitarian purpose. Sixth Street Bridge, one of the Trinity of Bridges, was built four times, from the wooden structure in 1819 to the present bow-type span built in 1928. The current design won first prize in an ISC Annual Bridge Award Competition as the most artistic bridge erected in 1928 in the U.S. and Canada. The glory was cut short when a scrappy county commissioner found a bridge of similar design over the Rhine River in Cologne, designed by Germans. His ramblings were cut just as short when the county clerk pointed out that the Sixth Street Bridge was copied from the Seventh Street Bridge, designed by a Pittsburgh architect who said it was a copy. In short, beauty need not be original.

Ninth Street Bridge completes the Trinity, a title applied to the three adjacent bridges for their matching designs. The predecessor of the Ninth Street Bridge enjoyed the distinction of a few good old stories. Armies crossing the bridge were required to break step because regularity of a march increased vibration and possible collapse. A local fiddle-maker asked for a block of timber from the old wooden arches when the city tore down the old bridge in 1890. Two violins were made, reputed to be unusually sweet in tone. According to the story, the violin-maker reasoned that the constant vibrations of the bridge over 50 years equalled many years of playing on a finished instrument.

George Westinghouse Memorial Bridge's 1,500-foot span between east Pittsburgh and Braddock over Turtle Creek Valley is nicknamed "Bridge of Size" for its $4,000,000 shortcut across the valley. Listed in *National Geographic* magazine in 1932, the bridge includes sculptured bas-reliefs on the four pylons depicting early historical events in steel, history, electricity, and transportation. Washington Crossing Memorial bridge at 40th Street recalls in its deck archways the trip Washington and a "Mr. Gist" made back from Fort LeBoeuf on foot, dressed as Indians. Washington fell into the icy waters as the pair crossed the Allegheny and Gist saved his life.

Bridges take Pittsburghers across the waters, but another ingenious contraption has pulled the city up the hills. Expansion south was limited to a narrow strip of flat land along the base of Mt. Washington. Steep slopes of 600 feet up Mt. Washington precluded building a road from the Monongahela to the top of the hill. Inclines, a sort of railroad car pulled up the hill, began scaling the slopes in 1854. The first, Kirk Lewis' Incline, hauled coal from mines near the top of Mt. Washington. In the next 30 years, some 20 more inclines of various types took people, coal, and goods up and down the surrounding hills. The Bellevue and Davis futilely relied on a storage battery to power the car up the hill electrically. By 1900, 17 inclines were operating on a daily basis.

Today, only two inclines remain in operation; the others are gone except to memories. The Monongahela incline rises 370 feet on a 640-foot-long track at an angle of 38 degrees up Mt. Washington. The incline can be boarded at its lower station on West Carson Street near the south end of Liberty Bridge or at its upper station on Grandview Avenue. Its steam-powered forerunner, built in 1870, was the second incline built in Pittsburgh, and the first to carry passengers. The present electrical version is owned and operated by the Port Authority of Allegheny County (PAT) and is a mainstay for hilltop residents who rely on public transportation, as well as a fun ride for tourists.

Private citizens recognized the value of the unique form of transport and rescued Duquesne Heights inclined plane in 1936. Owned by PAT, the cable railway has been restored and is operated by a non-profit citizen group. The group has reclaimed the beauty of the car's original handcarved cherry panels with birdseye maple trim, the amber glass transoms and handsome old hardware. The Dusquene incline has operated in perfect condition since 1877, although it is powered now by electricity instead of steam. More picturesque than The Old Mon, the Dusquene can be boarded at its restored upper station on Grandview Avenue or at its lower station on West Carson Street near the Fort Pitt Tunnel.

Demise of inclines was certain when people began piercing the hillsides with tunnels, making motor vehicle traffic easier. Residents opted for the automobile when the opening of Liberty Bridge and the Liberty Tubes through Mt. Washington opened the south side. The addition of the Fort Pitt tunnel broached another barrier and the incline succumbed to the automobile. Tunnels are nearly as prolific as bridges in Pittsburgh. Armstrong Tunnel still bears the soot of coal-powered industry, but students find it a good walking route to—or under—Duquesne University. And, with good old American ingenuity, when politics and money scuttled construction of another tunnel between the Liberty and Fort Pitt tunnels, the nearly-finished tunnel was converted to store the public buses.

Pittsburghers like almost anything old, particularly trolleys. Cold in the winter and hot in the summer, the early 20th-century mode of city travel is as evident as modern buses. Trolley tracks interrupt smooth pavement as often as cobblestones poke through the blacktop. Frequent talk of redoing the trolley system into an underground subway seems to fall on deaf ears, as Pittsburghers continue to rely on the clanking old trolleys. The spirit of The Renaissance hit even the trolleys with a fresh paint job. The bill for the dressing up was eased in a program that gave residents a chance to ''buy'' a trolley by purchasing advertising to select colors and designs for the exterior paint.